Milly, Molly

Beef

"We may look different
but we feel the same."

Milly and Molly are friends with everyone. All their friends are different and they all like different things.

Jack has shiny black hair and he loves carrots.

Meg has a lovely smile
and she's crazy about apples.

Harry has the whitest teeth
and he enjoys bananas.

Sophie has soft brown ringlets
and she just loves chocolate.

Tom has blue eyes
and he gets excited about blueberries.

Poppy has the longest braids
and strawberries are her favourites.

George has freckles
and can't walk past an orange.

Elizabeth has blonde curls
and she is mad about apricots.

And Humphrey...
Well, Humphrey just likes being a bully.

One day, for no good reason, Milly and Molly decided to make all their friends a special afternoon tea.

They made a carrot cake for Jack.

They made apple cakes for Meg...

and a banana cake for Harry.

They made a chocolate sponge cake for Sophie...

and blueberry muffins for Tom.

They made strawberry shortcake for Poppy...

and orange jelly for George.

They made an apricot upside-down cake
for Elizabeth...

and they even made gingerbread men for
Humphrey so as not to leave him out.

When there wasn't a crumb left, they decided
to go for a walk.

They walked all the way down to the end
of the lane where Farmer Hegarty kept
Beefy, the bull.

The opportunity was too much for Humphrey. He
did what Humphrey liked doing best...
being a bully!

Beefy watched quietly out of the corner
of his eye until suddenly he'd had enough.

The next day at school Humphrey was quiet.
In fact, he was very quiet. From that day
he never bullied again. Instead he was the
kindest friend and his favourite thing
was gingerbread.